I'm Reading About

INDIANA

The Hoosier State!

GALLOPADE

by Carole Marsh

Printed and Manufactured in Peachtree City, GA., USA
www.gallopade.com

Book design: John Hanson

Editorial manager: Janice Baker

Indiana is a great state.

It is one of a kind.

What makes Indiana special?

Let's read about it

and see!

NATIVE AMERICANS

Who lived in Indiana first?

Native Americans did!

They moved around to find food.
They hunted in Indiana's woods.
They fished in Indiana's rivers.
They gathered fruits and seeds and nuts.

EXPLORERS

The first explorers came to Indiana in 1679.
They came from the country of France.

Robert de La Salle was their leader.
He and his men were looking for new land!

SETTLEMENT

French people built many trading posts in Indiana.
One of the first trading posts was named Vincennes.
Today, Vincennes is the oldest city in Indiana!

Hunters could trade their animal furs for supplies at trading posts.

Vincennes
Vincennes

STATEHOOD

Indiana was the 19th state
to join the United States of America!

Isn't it great,
to be a state!
I bet Indiana
could hardly wait!

Indiana became a state in 1816.

Indiana
The 19th State
Here we are!

FLAG

I am the state flag.
I was adopted in 1917.

What colors am I?
Blue and gold.

Count my stars.
Look at me.
What else do you see?

I fly high over the state of Indiana!

INDIANA

CAPITAL

Say hello to Indianapolis,
the capital city of Indiana!

There is an important building in Indianapolis.
It is the Statehouse.
Indiana's laws are made there!

Statehouse

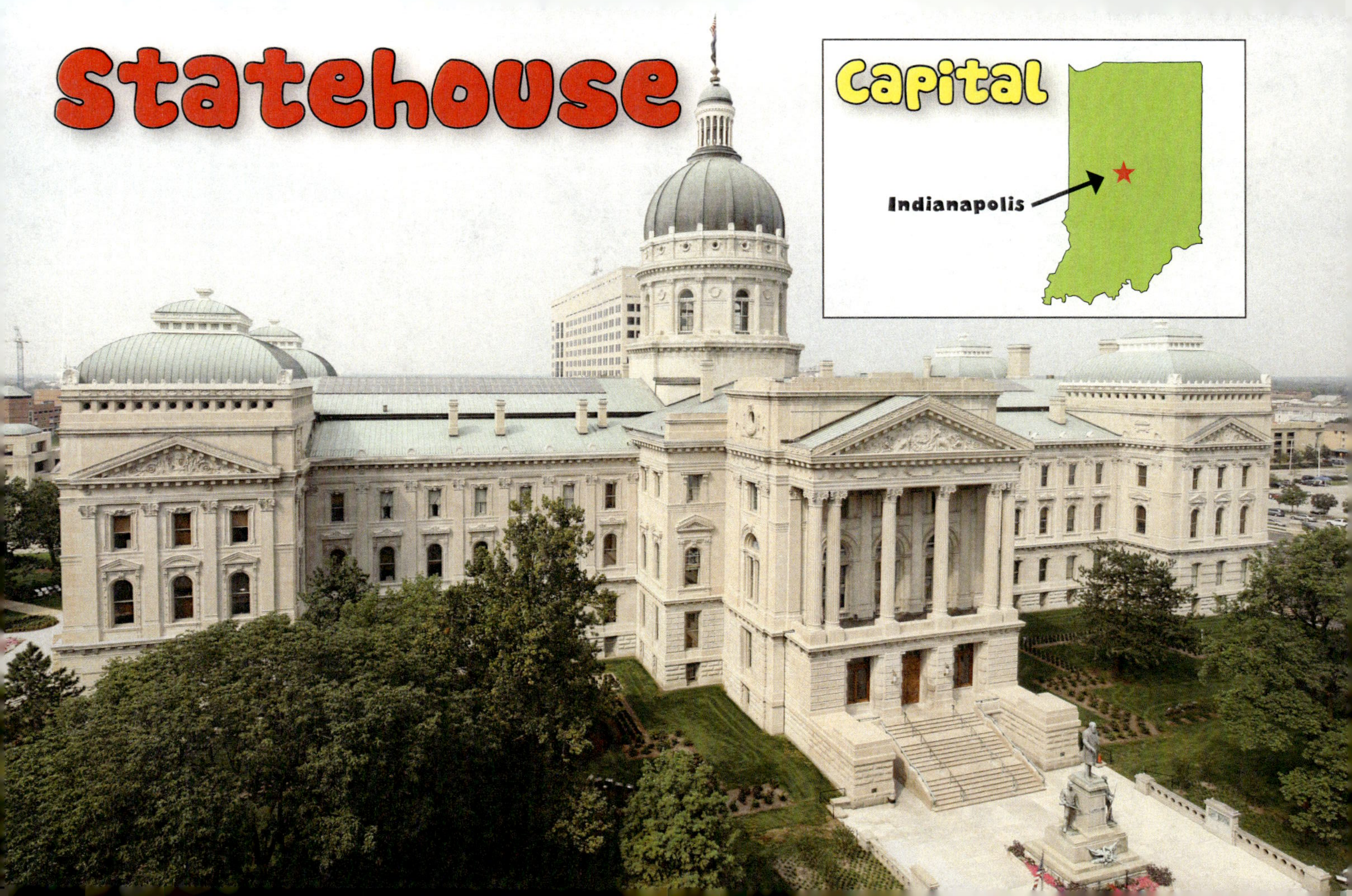

Capital

SEAL

I am a seal,
but I am not the State Seal.
If I were, I would be very important.
I would be stamped on many official papers.
(Ouch, that might hurt!)

SEAL OF THE STATE OF INDIANA
1816

Now, that's official!

NICKNAME

State nicknames are fun!
State nicknames are great!
They share fun facts
about each state!

Indiana's nickname is "The Hoosier State."

Indiana's first settlers were sometimes called Hoosiers.

The Hoosier State

BORDERS

Look at Indiana.
Indiana is in a region called "the Midwest."

Indiana borders four other states.
Find them on the map!

Borders

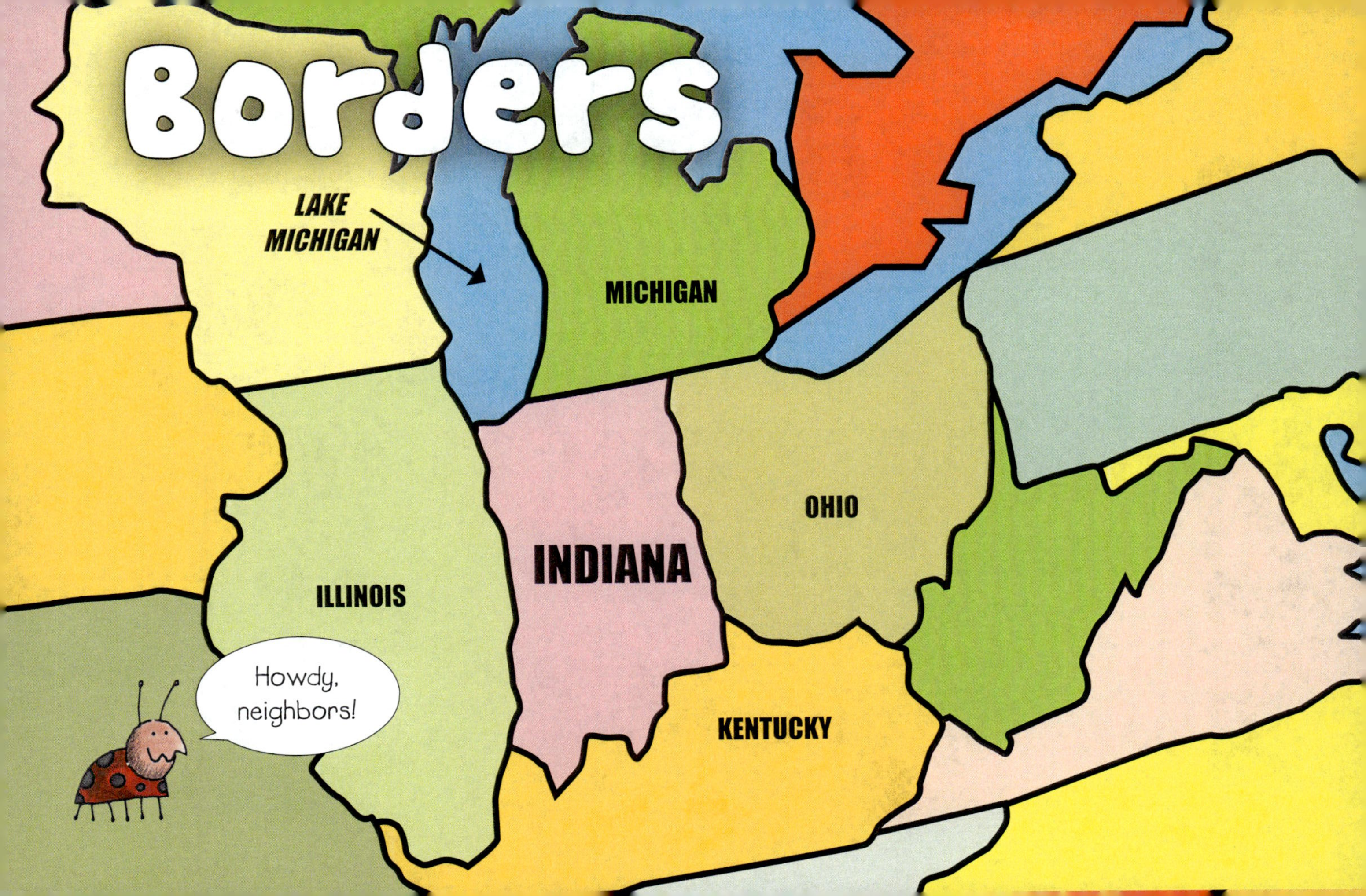
LAKE MICHIGAN
MICHIGAN
ILLINOIS
INDIANA
OHIO
KENTUCKY
Howdy, neighbors!

PRESIDENT

Benjamin Harrison was the 23rd President of the United States of America.
He lived in Indiana.

Benjamin grew up on a farm.
He liked to hunt and fish.
He went to school in a one-room schoolhouse.

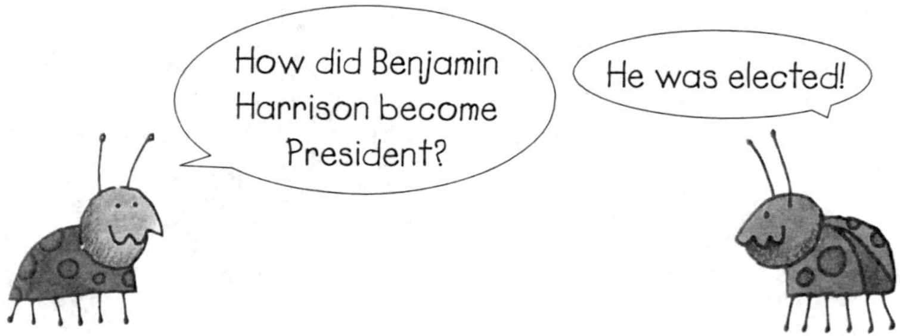

Benjamin Harrison

PEOPLE

Many famous people

Levi Coffin

Helped thousands of slaves escape on the Underground Railroad

Wilbur Wright

Invented the airplane with his brother Orville

Madame CJ Walker

Became a millionaire creating hair care products for black women

call our state home!

PEOPLE

Colonel Harland Sanders

Founder of Kentucky Fried Chicken

Jim Davis

Creator of the comic strip *Garfield*

Michael Jackson

Singer known as "The King of Pop"

Cardinal

BIRD

I am the state bird, and I fly
over Indiana, proud and high.

As I fly, up in the sky,
I flap my wings to tell you "Hi!"

The Indiana state bird is the Cardinal.

Peony

FLOWER

I am the Peony.
I am the state flower.

I grow where it's warm and sunny.
I bloom in spring and summer.
I help make Indiana beautiful!

Look at me! Smell me!
My petals are soft and pink!

Tulip Tree

TREE

I am a Tulip Tree—I'm the state tree.
All over Indiana is where to find me.

My roots run deep, they keep me strong.
I can live for hundreds of years—that's very long!

I stand up straight, big and tall.
Don't climb too high—it would hurt to fall!

Salem Limestone

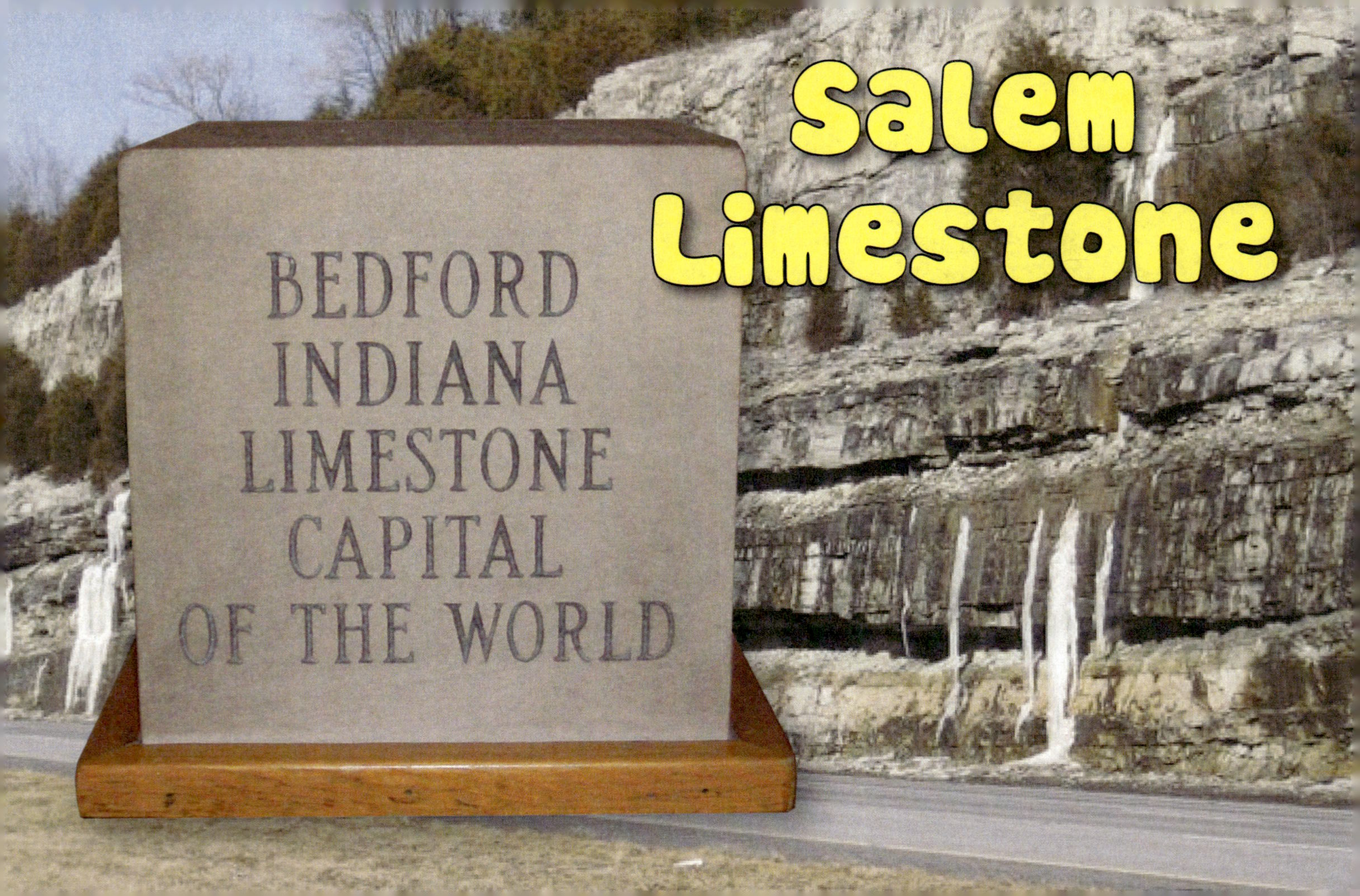

ROCK

I am Salem Limestone.
I am the state rock.
I am found all over southern Indiana.

I was discovered by Native Americans.
Settlers used me to make their homes.

Indiana's Statehouse was built with Salem limestone!

Lake Michigan
The fish are biting today!

LAKES

Let's go to the lake!

We can wade in the water.
We can ride on a boat.

We can jump off the dock
onto an inner tube float!

Lake Michigan, Indiana's Great Lake, is home to many animals:

Fish **Snakes** **Birds** **Turtles** **Salamanders** **and More!**

Caves

CAVES

Indiana has many caves.
They are dark and wet.
You can explore them if you're brave!

Salem limestone is smooth and flat.
It lines the walls of the caves.
Be careful, you might see a bat!

Rivers

RIVERS

Indiana has many rivers.
People like to use rivers for boating and fishing!

This habitat is home to many animals:

Birds Deer Snakes Frogs Fish and More!

Rivers were Indiana's first highways. Many settlers to Indiana came down the Ohio River on flatboats.

Santa Claus
Merry Christmas!
And a Happy New Year!
-Welcome To-
Santa Claus
Indiana
America's Christmas Hometown

LANDMARK

Santa Claus is a town in Indiana.
Children send letters to Santa Claus every Christmas.
Thousands of letters arrive in the town.

Santa Claus has a theme park called Holiday World. You can celebrate Christmas every day in Santa Claus!

Indiana Crops

AGRICULTURE

Indiana has many farms.
Why?
Because Indiana has good soil and a mild climate!

Some of the top crops grown in Indiana are:

Corn Soybeans Hay Wheat

Hey!
Don't forget about me!
I am a hog from Indiana.
Indiana farms raise lots of hogs!

Oink! Oink!

Sports in Indiana

SPORTS

Baseball! Basketball! Football!
Indiana has it all.

Whether you like to watch or play,
You are sure to have a ball!

Colts **Firebirds** **Pacers**

Hoosiers **Boilermakers**

Fighting Irish

& More!

Indiana: Home of the Indianapolis Motor Speedway

CLAIM TO FAME

The Indianapolis Motor Speedway is a famous racetrack.
It is used for automobile races.
Racecars can go more than 200 miles per hour on the Speedway!

The Indy 500 is the most famous race run at the Speedway.

GLOSSARY

climate: weather conditions in an area over a long period of time

elect: to choose someone by voting

flatboat: a boat with a flat bottom and square ends used to carry goods and people on rivers

habitat: a place where plants or animals naturally live

region: an area that has similar characteristics

settlement: the first community in an area

spelunking: exploring caves

Underground Railroad: a network of people and safe houses used to help slaves escape from the South to the North in the 1800s